Presented to:

_____

From:

_____

Date:

_____

DEVOTIONS
FOR THE
Fall

Stacy Edwards

THOMAS NELSON

Since 1798

Introduction

*E*ven when I was a child, fall was always my favorite time of year. There was something about bobbing for apples, going on hayrides, and wearing soft sweaters that brought me such joy. I loved every cool breeze, colored leaf, and caramel apple. While most of my friends were counting down the days until they received Christmas presents, I preferred the fall months, which were more about the presence of family. Fall had all the good foods, without any of the pressure of finding just the right gift for cousin so-and-so.

I still remember sneaking away from the kids' table at family gatherings, slipping into the kitchen to hear an aunt or uncle tell the same story they had told every year for as long as I could remember, and everyone laughing as if they'd never heard it before. For me, fall meant family, and family felt really good. Looking back, I realize how many gifts God gave me throughout the years. I'm so grateful for every pumpkin we ever carved, every festival we ever attended, and every "Trick or treat!" I ever uttered. I wasn't as grateful for the corduroy pantsuit I got one year, but that's another story entirely. Let's just say it itched beyond belief.

Fall brings out a little of the child in all of us. We all have some memories attached to the season, whether tied to a scent, a certain food, or a specific activity. Maybe it's a hint of cinnamon, the taste of pumpkin, or the sight of a corn maze that transports us to another time, when life seemed a little simpler and family enveloped us like a warm coat on a cold day. When I think of falls past, I see the Lord's goodness in my life on full display.

My prayer is that somewhere in these pages you will be reminded of the goodness of God in your own life. Perhaps you will recall a memory that you've not thought of in some time. Maybe you'll think of someone special, and it will bring a smile to your face. It could be that God reveals Himself to you in a whole new way through the simple gifts of this season.

I hope the words written here point you to the Father, who loves you dearly and is the Source of every good and perfect gift (James 1:17). Even now, I'm thinking of baking cookies with my grandma, jumping in leaves with my brother, and watching my own children gather with cousins, as I once did.

God is so kind to us. He is generous with His goodness. You are so very loved, and I pray you feel it today. Grab some hot cocoa and enjoy.

Stacy Edwards

First Fall Breeze

Repent therefore and be converted, that your sins
may be blotted out, so that times of refreshing
may come from the presence of the Lord.

Acts 3:19

You think it will never happen as you perspire your way through the dog days of summer. When the fans run full blast and there isn't enough sweet tea in the world to quench your thirst. The pavement is hot, the air is thick, and the mosquitoes outnumber the people. You begin operating in survival mode, believing that, maybe, this will actually be the year when it doesn't show up.

Then, one morning, you step outside onto your front porch, and you feel it. There's something different in the air—a coolness that tells you fall has finally arrived. There's a crispness to the wind that invigorates you as the burdensome heat of summer fades away. Your heart is lightened, and your spirit is revived. There isn't anything quite as refreshing as that first fall breeze that announces the arrival of a new season.

Our lives go through seasons, just like the calendar. There are periods when we feel weary from the weight of our sins. The guilt and shame we carry are as oppressive as the heat of a Southern July day. There seems to be no end in sight, and we find ourselves just trying to survive. That is not the life our heavenly Father desires for His children. Thankfully, just as we turn a calendar page, we can turn from the heaviness of our former ways.

Just like that first fall breeze, repentance will bring a refreshing new season into our lives. When we turn from our sins and turn toward Jesus, forgiveness blows over us like a crisp autumn wind, and new energy is instilled in us. The sky is a little brighter, the colors are a little bolder, and our steps are a little lighter as the burden is lifted.

Walking in freedom with Jesus is as stimulating as that first fall breeze. Everything that once weighed us down just falls away, and a fresh beginning is ours for the taking. Everything is brimming with possibility, and the opportunities are endless. Let's repent, be refreshed, and embrace a new season with Christ.

Gather *together.*

2

Haunted Houses

*"I give them eternal life, and they shall never perish;
neither shall anyone snatch them out of My hand."*

John 10:28

hen I was a teenager, I went with my parents to Pigeon
Forge, Tennessee, for a fall getaway. We walked up
and down the main strip and breathed in all the scents of
funnel cakes, homemade fudge, and smoked sausage. We
entered every shop selling wooden wind chimes and leather
goods. At one point, we found ourselves standing outside of
a haunted house.

On a whim, my parents paid their hard-earned money
for us to enter a dark building where strangers would jump
out from behind closed doors in an attempt to give us

nightmares for the rest of our lives. Inside, one of these dark figures called me by name and reached out as if to snatch me away. We were greatly relieved when we made our way to the exit and once again found ourselves standing safely outside of that building.

As we stood on the sidewalk, discussing the terrifying experience, an employee of the haunted house told me, "It's not as scary once you know that they aren't allowed to physically touch you." What I discovered was that the people could dress as scary as they wanted. They could moan, groan, and reach for me, but they had their limits. There were boundaries they couldn't cross. For all their threats and taunts, the guests walking in their midst were untouchable to them.

This world can feel like a haunted house, complete with shadowy figures, dead ends, and unpleasant surprises around the corner. We can feel the hot breath of the Enemy on the backs of our necks and begin to wonder if we'll make it out. But we must remember that, just like those haunted-house employees, Satan has boundaries that he can't cross.

As Christ followers, we enjoy the protection of God the Father. We are held safely and securely in the palm of His hand. The Enemy can present himself as scary as he wants. He can moan, groan, and reach for us. But for all his threats and taunts, we walk in this world knowing that we belong to God and can never be snatched away from Him.

Oh, how great is Your *goodness*,
which You have laid up for those who fear You,
which You have prepared for those who trust in
You in the presence of the sons of men!

PSALMS 31:19

3

Cinnamon Brooms

*Walk in love, as Christ also has loved us
and given Himself for us, an offering and a
sacrifice to God for a sweet-smelling aroma.*

Ephesians 5:2

It was the ultimate act of love when Christ laid down His life for us. Paul said that it was a sweet smell to the Father. I've often wondered about the aroma of such an extravagant sacrifice. How would one even describe the scent of selfless love? There's no way for us to know the specific formulation—its top and base notes—of that fragrance, but when we walk in love, God smells it all over again. He breathes in every act of service, kind word, and offering of grace, and it reminds Him of Jesus.

Scents can be such powerful things; one sniff can take us back to a different place in time. The right aroma can completely change our mind-sets and lift our spirits. For me, the presence of cinnamon brooms near the checkout at the grocery store will always signal the beginning of the fall and holiday season.

I don't know why, when thinking of something to infuse with the scent of cinnamon, someone decided a broom was the thing, but I'm all for it. Cinnamon brooms make me happy and conjure up all sorts of pleasant memories. They will always make me think of fall mantels, chili on the stove, and family gatherings. Wherever I've found myself in life and whatever I've gone through, one whiff of those brooms and I'm reminded of the good times.

Paul said that Christ followers are the fragrance of Christ both to the saved and to the perishing (2 Corinthians 2:15). Just as a cinnamon broom brings reminders of fall festivities, our lives should serve as a reminder of Jesus' life and love. One whiff, so to speak, should remind people of the love that the heavenly Father poured out on His children.

Don't we want our lives to be like that? Imagine our heavenly Father watching us walk in love and savoring the sweet-smelling aroma. Imagine the way we live reminding people that they are loved. Let's make it our aim in life to walk as Jesus walked and to leave the scent of love everywhere we go.

Apple
of my eye

4

The Fireplace Mantel

There is a time for everything, and a season
for every activity under the heavens.

Ecclesiastes 3:1 NIV

The fireplace mantel sets the tone for the entire home. Live plants, birdcages, or greenery would indicate that spring has arrived. Garland with lights, gingerbread men, and snow scenes hint at the Christmas season. Then, of course, there is the crème de la crème of home decor—the fall mantel. There is nothing like the colorful leaves, pumpkins, and pine cones to bring all the cozy vibes into your home.

The thing about the fall mantel, though, is that you have to wait patiently for the appropriate time to reveal it. You may be pining for cooler temps in August, but you can't put the pine cones out until the weather and the calendar have both declared it to be autumn. There is no forcing one season to give way to another; it simply happens when it's supposed to happen. You embrace the season you're in, and then, one morning, you wake to realize that a new season has begun.

Just like a fireplace mantel, our lives look different depending on the season in which we find ourselves. Some of us are chasing careers, while others are adjusting to retirement. There are those rocking babies and those releasing young adults out into the world. There are single folks, empty nesters, and senior caregivers, and there can be fruitfulness in every season. Maybe you used to serve your church in a variety of ways, but now your age or health has limited you. It's okay; you're just in a new season. God knows and can use you in new ways.

Scripture tells us that there is a time for everything under heaven. God is aware of our current season, and we don't need to feel the pressure to rush from one to the next. There will come a time when we are ready to put the pumpkins away and dress our mantels anew. A new season will bring fresh beauty to our homes. In much the same way, God moves us from one season of life to the next, and one can be just as fruitful as the next.

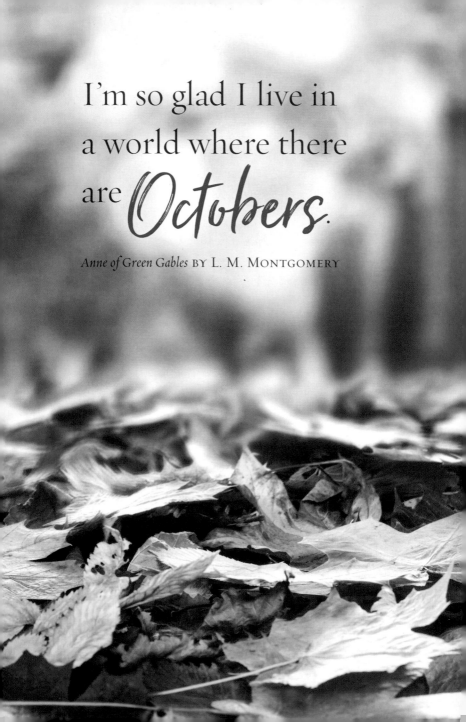

I'm so glad I live in a world where there are *Octobers.*

Anne of Green Gables BY L. M. MONTGOMERY

5

Pumpkin of Thankfulness

Oh, give thanks to the LORD, for He is
good! For His mercy endures forever.

1 Chronicles 16:34

Gratitude should be a hallmark of God's people. If we were to consistently count our blessings, it would be a never-ending endeavor. Yet, too often, we become distracted and fail to acknowledge any of the gifts we've been given. Life becomes hectic, and countless gifts from the Father pass by us unnoticed. We allow life to overwhelm us, and our grumbling overshadows our gratitude.

A beautiful by-product of the fall season is the tendency

to refocus our hearts on thankfulness. There is something about the cooler temperatures and approaching holidays that helps us refocus our hearts on what matters. We find ourselves pausing to reflect and take stock of all that God has done in our lives. One tangible way we can do this is to implement a pumpkin of thankfulness into our fall traditions.

The idea behind the pumpkin of thankfulness is simple. You place a pumpkin and a permanent marker in a prominent location in your home. Each day you write on the pumpkin a blessing God has given you. It might be a person He has brought into your life, an answer to a specific prayer, or something as simple as a sunny day. By Thanksgiving you should have a pumpkin full of reasons to be grateful. Perhaps you'll even wish you had used a bigger pumpkin.

It's easy to get caught up in our trials and troubles and lose sight of our blessings. That is why we are told countless times in Scripture to remember what the Lord has done for us. We are to tell our children and grandchildren about the goodness of the Lord. And we are to continually thank Him for all that we've been given.

We will discover that being grateful will guard our hearts against envy, bitterness, and all manner of unpleasantness in our lives. Counting our blessings reminds us of how much our heavenly Father cares for us. Let's make a point of being grateful this season, and we may as well use a pumpkin!

Hello, *fall!*

6

The Acorn Wreath

"I will give you a new heart and put a new spirit
within you; I will take the heart of stone out
of your flesh and give you a heart of flesh."

Ezekiel 36:26

*I*f you spend any time on social media during the fall season, you will see an endless stream of autumn crafts. And
many of them are wreaths. Everything from kernels of corn
to pine cones can be hot glued onto an oval frame and hung
on a front door. Even the least crafty of us feel inspired to
create something.

One year my children made me the prettiest wreath out
of acorns. They had worked so diligently to hot glue dozens,
if not hundreds, of tiny acorns together. They presented it

to me with all the pride a couple of kids can muster. So, with an equal amount of pride, I laid the wreath on my dining room table and used it as a candleholder. It was so lovely . . . for a time.

I'm going to let you in on a little secret regarding acorn wreaths. You have to bake the acorns first. This step isn't always listed on those lovely DIY blogs. It turns out that insects like to live in acorns, and you must remove them. This means that if you, hypothetically, use a wreath made from unbaked acorns as a candleholder on your dining room table, all kinds of unpleasantness will ensue.

When we come to God, the first thing He must do is empty us of all the unpleasantness that lives in our hearts. And we must repent and let go of all the things that have taken up residence within us. Otherwise it's only a matter of time before what is in us comes out. We may be quick to become angry when we don't get our way. Perhaps we are prone to gossip or deception. Maybe we give in and return to old patterns of sin when things become difficult.

The beautiful thing about coming to Christ is He is not repulsed by our inner uncleanliness. He knows exactly how to remove what needs to be removed so we can be made into something beautiful for Him. Let's allow the Lord to deal with whatever is in our hearts so that we can be the new creations He has called us to become.

And let the *peace* of God rule in your hearts, to which also you were called in one body; and be *thankful*.

COLOSSIANS 3:15

7

A Cornucopia

The fruit of the Spirit is love, joy, peace,
longsuffering, kindness, goodness,
faithfulness, gentleness, self-control.
Against such [things] there is no law.

Galatians 5:22-23

When I think of the fruit of the Spirit, I imagine the cornucopia my mother used to set out in our home around Thanksgiving. I can still picture the wicker basket that lay on its side and the plastic fruits and vegetables spilling out of it. As a child, I would often want to play with the individual pieces of fruit, but it wasn't possible to remove just one element from the centerpiece. The food was all glued together into one inseparable mass of goodness.

In my mind, the fruit of the Spirit works much the same way. We aren't offered peace on Tuesdays and patience on Thursdays. We don't pick and choose which fruit we will enjoy or exhibit to others on any given day. They are all mingled together and overflowing in our lives on a daily basis. They are a beautiful and inseparable mass of goodness in the life of a believer.

The very definition of *cornucopia* aptly describes the fruit of the Spirit. According to Encyclopedia.com, a cornucopia is "an abundant supply of good things." That is exactly what our heavenly Father instills in us when we come to Him. We are filled with an abundant supply of all the good things the Holy Spirit has to offer. There are too many gifts to hold, so they spill out of us as we interact with others. Whatever is within us comes out in our actions and attitudes.

While a cornucopia may come out only in the fall, we can have love, patience, kindness, and gentleness toward others no matter the season of life or circumstances. We can experience joy, peace, faithfulness, and self-control within ourselves every day of the year. And all these things are mingled together and overflowing in such a way that it is evident to those around us. Our lives are a cornucopia filled with gifts from the Father.

5 Ways to Create a Cozy Vibe in Your Home

* **Soft** blankets
* Chunky pillows
* Scented **candles**
* Hot beverages
* Reading material within reach

8

Friday-Night Lights

Aspire to lead a quiet life, to mind your
own business, and to work with your
own hands, as we commanded you.

1 Thessalonians 4:11

*E*verything about life has become a little more complicated these days. Our schedules, our relationships, and even our entertainment seem to take more effort and energy than they used to require. Social media has us critiquing every movement while entirely missing the moment. Isn't it exhausting to live that way? We all secretly long for something simpler but aren't sure how to achieve it.

One Friday night, after another round of "I don't know, dear. What do *you* want to do tonight?" my husband suggested we go to a local high school football game. That night we sat beneath the stadium lights, each enjoying a hot dog and a fountain drink. We cheered for the home team and sat a little closer when the night air became cold. As we drove home that evening, we declared it to be the best date we'd had in a long time.

When Paul wrote his first letter to the Thessalonians, he encouraged them to seek to live a simple life. Apparently, even back then, people needed a reminder that they could give up their seats on the crazy train and return to a quieter way of living. Live a quiet life. Mind your own business. Work with your hands. Those were not suggestions but commands Paul gave to the people for their own benefit.

The fall season is the perfect time to step back and evaluate the way we've been living. Have we spent the summer scurrying to and fro? Are we exhausted from trying to entertain ourselves? Do we focus too much on how other people are living while our own lives pass us by? It's so easy to get caught up in what we think the good life looks like. Let's give all of that up.

Let's seek a quiet life. Let's mind our own business and keep our hands busy. Don't rush through the beauty of this season. What things do we need to remove from our calendars to create some free space? If you need a starting place for the simple life, I strongly suggest the Friday-night lights of a high school football game.

Pick of the *patch*

9

Corn Mazes

Jesus said to him, "I am the way, the truth, and the
life. No one comes to the Father except through Me."

John 14:6

*N*othing says "fall in the South" quite like getting lost in a good old-fashioned corn maze. Farmers go through a lot of planning and work to create these intricately designed labyrinths. What begins as lighthearted fall fun for the partakers can, however, produce a little panic after a certain point. The numerous and seemingly identical paths will, as the sun begins to set, bring to mind every scary movie that ever involved a cornfield. The most important thing to remember about a corn maze is this: there is only one way out.

When Jesus told the disciples that He was going to prepare a place for them after He went away, Thomas became concerned. "We do not know where You are going," he said. "How can we know the way?" (John 14:5). How confusing it must have been for Thomas. After all, there weren't any maps to this place Jesus was going. Jesus informed Thomas that there was only one way, and it was through Him. He is the way. He is the truth. He is life. No one is able to come to the Father except through Jesus, the Son.

The world wants it to work differently. "You do you" is the battle cry of the day. People are being deceived into believing that whatever makes them happy is what is best for them. Still others are told that there are many ways to heaven, which stands in direct opposition to what Scripture teaches. There are many people today who are lost and searching for the way out, and we hold the map.

Just as in a proper corn maze, there is only one way to freedom, and that is through Jesus. It is the job of those of us who have discovered it to lead others there as well. Let's seek out the stragglers, wave to those still wandering, and help guide them all home. Let's meet them on their dead-end trail, if necessary, and walk with them to the right path. May no one come into our lives and leave without hearing about the one and only way out.

I will praise the name
of God with a *song*,
and will magnify
Him with *thanksgiving*.

PSALM 69:30

10

Falling Leaves

Let all bitterness, wrath, anger, clamor, and evil
speaking be put away from you, with all malice.

Ephesians 4:31

*P*eople wait for them with great anticipation, families plan entire vacations around them, and children squeal with delight at the sight of them. Who among us doesn't feel a little jolt of joy when we witness the trees finally letting go of their leaves? We realize, as we watch them dance in the wind, that there is something incredibly beautiful and freeing about letting things go. It causes us to hold loosely to things and to realize that many things the world deems important don't really matter.

In his letter to the Ephesians, Paul instructed the

recipients to let go of bitterness, anger, hard feelings, envy, and slanderous speech. He knew that negative thoughts, emotions, and actions weigh a person down. It is terribly difficult to navigate life carrying that kind of baggage, and it affects every area of our existence. It may seem obvious that these hinder the kind of life we long to live, yet how many of us are often guilty of clinging to those very things?

Perhaps we feel protected by our grudges, and that is why we hold on to our anger as to a shield. Maybe we fear being exposed and vulnerable, so we hide behind hard feelings and keep others at a distance with harsh words. We probably think we are doing ourselves a favor, but if we would loosen our grip, beautiful things would happen. Pain would begin to fall away, and peace would take its place. Grudges would be replaced by grace. We would learn to travel lighter.

Let's take a moment this fall to watch and learn from the falling leaves. Let's witness the way they spin and twirl as the breeze carries them far away. May they serve as a reminder to us of the freedom of letting things go. We, too, can experience the lightness that comes when dying things, like bitterness and anger, fall away. Choosing to release our hold on negative thoughts and emotions is every bit as beautiful as falling leaves. What shall we let go of today?

Football, bonfires, and hayrides

II

Pralines

But if we hope for what we do not see, we
eagerly wait for it with perseverance.

Romans 8:25

Pralines are a lovely treat for fall and, in our home, mark the onset of the holiday season. If you've been fortunate enough to eat them, you know that they are absolutely delicious. And if you were to look at a recipe for pralines, you would be amazed at the simplicity of the ingredients. There is sugar, more sugar, butter, vanilla, and pecans. It would seem to the casual observer that anyone could make pralines.

Here is what one must realize before embarking on a praline-making adventure: they take some serious perseverance. The recipe is quite misleading when it says, "Stir until mixture thickens." Spoiler alert: you're going to be stirring for a sweet forever. Many who attempt to make the sticky-sweet goodies will give up. They will walk away before the finished product is revealed. But perseverance results in a perfect praline.

In the book of Romans, Paul wrote to believers concerning the future glories promised to them. He said that they must hope for it with certainty, even though they could not see it with their eyes at the moment. They were to wait for it with expectation and perseverance, knowing that the result would be worth the effort. His words were an encouragement to not give up or walk away.

We sometimes misunderstand Scripture. We read about heaven and the future promised to us. We know that we are to repent and believe, and it seems like a simple recipe for a happy life. Paul had walked the road as a Christ disciple, and he knew the hard work and discipline it took. So he encouraged the Romans to persevere, to not quit, and to finish the race.

When making pralines, you can't give up. You must stir, stir, and stir. At the proper moment the mixture will, in fact, thicken. Likewise, followers of Christ must continue to do the work of a disciple. We must continue to pray, work, and tell others about the goodness of the grace of God. Then, at the proper time, we will receive the thing for which we have hoped and persevered. We will stand in the presence of Jesus.

5 Fall Activities for Kids

* Carve a *pumpkin*
* Visit a corn maze
* Go *apple* picking
* Jump in leaves
* Take a hayride

12

Wassail

Now to Him who is able to do exceedingly
abundantly above all that we ask or think . . .

Ephesians 3:20

The majority of us unknowingly settle for far less than our heavenly Father desires to give us. We are cherished by the Creator of the universe, who longs to lavish us with good things. He has an endless storehouse of peace, joy, and blessings, yet we fail to access most of it. We struggle, strive, and wonder what we're doing wrong. We ask so little of a God who is the Creator and controller of all that has ever existed.

Every year, around October, wassail begins to make appearances at family gatherings, church socials, and even some higher-end retail stores. The aroma entices you, and the taste never disappoints.

One year, in an effort to bring the amazing fall beverage into my home, I purchased some apple cider and cinnamon sticks. While the smell was lovely, something was missing from the overall experience. I wanted to enjoy wassail, but I was clearly doing something wrong.

Then I went to an event where someone who was known for her wassail brought it for everyone to enjoy. One mug of that divine warmth and I realized I had been settling for far less than apple cider had to offer. I had to discover the secret and find out what I had been doing incorrectly. It turns out that if you add some brown sugar, cloves, and frozen orange juice, ordinary, run-of-the-mill cider becomes the holiday delight known as wassail.

Once a person has had a properly made wassail, she can never go back to being satisfied with a couple of cinnamon sticks floating in some cider. Even more so, once someone realizes the unlimited peace, love, and joy available to him in Christ, he can never go back to trying to do things on his own and attempting to maintain control of his life. When we say to the Lord, "Not my will, but Thine," we open ourselves up to receive more than we could have even thought to ask. Then we will never again be content settling for less.

Ms. Paulette's Wassail

1 gallon apple cider

½ cup light brown sugar

4 cinnamon sticks

20 whole cloves

1 (12-ounce) container frozen orange juice
    concentrate

½ cup lemon juice

Combine the apple cider, brown sugar, cinnamon sticks, and cloves in a large pot. Bring to a boil; then simmer for 10 minutes. Strain. Add the orange juice concentrate and lemon juice and stir until liquid is warm.

Leaves are falling, and **autumn** is calling.

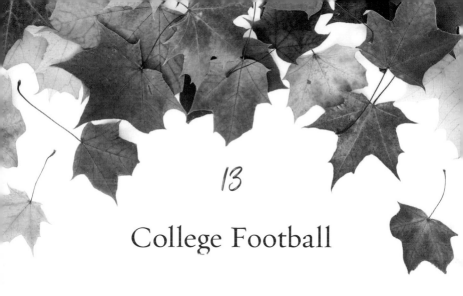

13

College Football

For our citizenship is in heaven, from which we also
eagerly wait for the Savior, the Lord Jesus Christ.

Philippians 3:20

*I*t doesn't matter where you currently live when it comes
to college football. If there's one thing my father has
taught me, it's that you always root for your hometown
team. Even though I have lived in several states, for instance,
I will always cheer for the Buckeyes. My husband, on the
other hand, will always cheer for the LSU Tigers because
his people call Louisiana home. Home is always home even
when you aren't physically there.

An amazing thing happens when we make a commit-
ment to follow Christ. We become citizens of another place.

Our home is now heaven, and earth is only a place we are passing through. We find ourselves a little less comfortable in this world and a little more homesick for the one to come. An understanding of where we're from changes the way we live. We can approach any valley knowing that it is simply a pit stop. Also, we view any mountaintop experience through the lens of our eternal home that awaits us.

Where we consider ourselves "from" is a large part of our identity. Think about it. Home shapes everything from our taste in food to our music preferences. It affects how we speak and how comfortable we are interacting with our neighbors. It certainly has a great deal to do with which college team we root for on fall weekends.

As Christ followers, we call heaven our home, and it shapes everything about us. We act, think, and speak differently because of where we call home. We love others better, forgive a little faster, and consider others as more important than ourselves.

Like a Southern drawl, a certain style of pizza, or our favorite college team, there are always things about us that hint at where we are from. As Christians, our lives are marked by our faith in Jesus, our love for one another, and our hope of heaven. Everything about us sets us apart as different and as from another place. All of these things give us away in the best possible way.

14

Fall Clothing

Preach the word! Be ready in season and
out of season. Convince, rebuke, exhort,
with all longsuffering and teaching.

2 Timothy 4:2

*I*t happens to many of us every year. As summer winds
down, we know we need to review our family's ward-
robe. We need to ensure that, though we've been living in
shorts and sandals, we also have sweaters and boots when
necessary. Yet it's often difficult to think about such things
in the sweltering days of August. Summers seem endless,
don't they? So we put off what we know we ought to do and,
inevitably, regret it.

We awake one morning to a chill in the air and, perhaps,

some frost on the ground. Only then do we realize that we never did properly prepare. We desperately search the backs of closets, hoping our children can still wear last year's coats and praying everyone hasn't outgrown last fall's shoes. The fact is, fall's arrival isn't the best time to prepare for it. Preparation, by its very definition, is done in advance. This is hard for those of us whose default response is procrastination.

In his second letter to Timothy, Paul instructed him to be prepared to preach the Word in convenient and inconvenient seasons. Timothy was to be prepared for the changing of seasons. Likewise, we must be prepared spiritually for every season in life. Once a trial or tragedy is upon us, it's too late to begin preparing for it. We, as believers, must know what we believe to be true about God before the cold season arrives. We need to be certain beforehand of what Scripture says about Him and His love for us.

We make it far harder on ourselves when we enter a difficult season unprepared. Let's take a moment today and consider what we know to be true of our God. What has He taught us about Himself? What truths and promises would bring us strength, comfort, and encouragement in the midst of pain and persecution? Knowing these things is one way we can prepare ourselves for the changing of seasons that we know will arrive. Let's not be caught off guard when the cold winds begin to blow.

That I may proclaim with the voice of thanksgiving, and tell of all Your *Wondrous* works.

PSALMS 26:7

Simply *blessed*

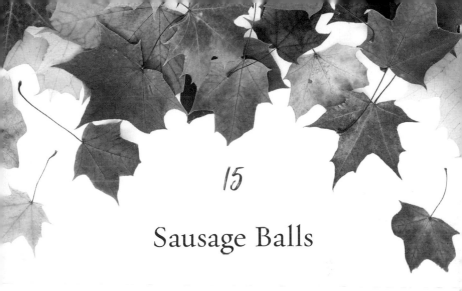

15

Sausage Balls

Above all these things put on love,
which is the bond of perfection.

Colossians 3:14

If you've ever been to a social gathering in the fall, then you've been introduced to the sausage ball. It seems incredibly simple. It involves ground pork sausage (spicy, if you dare), cheese, and some biscuit baking mix. Seriously, that's all. Oh, sure, there are recipes out there that will suggest all sorts of things, from cilantro to cayenne. But all you truly need are the three ingredients I named.

When I first attempted to make sausage balls, I used only sausage and cheese. I didn't realize there was a third and very important ingredient. It turned out that the baking mix was key to a successful outcome because it was the binding agent. It didn't matter how delicious the sausage or how fresh the cheese. The binding agent was absolutely essential. Without it, everything else falls apart, and no one wants to serve a platter of deconstructed sausage balls to their guests.

In his letter to the Colossians, Paul gave some specific instructions. Believers were to be merciful, kind, and humble. They were told to be patient with and forgiving of one another. Their lives were to be marked by meekness and kindness. How were they to accomplish these things? How could Paul have possibly expected them to be patient with people whom they found difficult? What would it take for a person to forgive someone who, perhaps, wasn't even sorry? There has to be something in a person that would make this sort of living possible.

Living a godly life requires a binding agent. It calls for, above all else, love. It is love for God and love for one another that enables us to conduct ourselves with patience, meekness, and kindness. It is the love of Jesus bubbling up within us that causes us to forgive one another and tolerate differences within the context of the Christian community. Without love, everything else will crumble like a poorly constructed sausage ball. So, as we strive to live godly lives, let's be sure to bind it all together with love.

Enter into His gates with
thanksgiving, and into
His courts with *praise*.
Be thankful to Him, and
bless His name

PSALM 100:4

16

Sunny but Cold

"Beware of false prophets, who come to you in sheep's
clothing, but inwardly they are ravenous wolves."

Matthew 7:15

There is a warning found in Scripture regarding those who would appear to be followers of Christ but who would, in fact, be against Him. The imagery is intense and intended to put us on the offensive. We are told that these individuals appear to be as gentle and innocent as sheep. Yet for those deceived enough to get too close, they discover them to be ravenous wolves. What an unpleasant surprise.

Appearances can be deceiving. It happens often in the early fall months of the year. You will look out of your window to see bright sunshine and blue skies. Your heart will dance just a little, especially if the weather has been gloomy for a few days. You head outside, expecting to feel the warmth of the sun on your skin, but instead you feel the bite of a frigid fall wind.

It turns out that things (and people) are not always what they seem. God's Word refers more than once to the need for His people to use discernment when dealing with others. It is especially important when dealing with those who claim to be teaching or preaching the Word of God. What initially sounds appealing may be in direct opposition to what Scripture teaches.

The key is to use wisdom and discernment when determining which teachings we will follow. It is wise to do what the Bereans did when listening to Paul's teachings (Acts 17:11). They were quick to take what they heard and compare it to God's Word. This prevented them from being deceived

We can't assume that someone speaks the truth just because they look the part and speak with authority. A person can't be judged by the size of their platform or their number of followers. Those man-made metrics can lead us astray. They may be a great storyteller but not a truth teller. Just as the sun may shine brightly yet the day still be cold, false teachers can trick us if we aren't careful.

5 Tips for Fall Gatherings

* A Make-Your-Own-*Hot-Cocoa* bar with cinnamon sticks, whipped topping, caramel drizzle, peppermint extract, and so on.

* Ask everyone to bring a nonperishable food item for a local pantry.

* Watch a football game together.

* Have a good, old fashioned *pajama party.*

17

Bonfires

*"Let your light so shine before men, that they may see
your good works and glorify your Father in heaven."*

Matthew 5:16

We live in a world that is often darkened by brokenness
and sin. If we listened to many of the voices of the
world, we would be tempted to believe that there isn't any
light left at all. Media outlets often paint a picture of doom
and gloom. It would become quite distressing if we were to
believe it. But if we stop to look around, we will see that there
are sparks of light everywhere, and the world isn't as dark as
it sometimes seems.

Our job as Christ followers is to focus on and follow
Him. We are to keep our eyes straight ahead and to walk as

He walked. When we do that, we won't be able to help but shine a light everywhere we go. "This little light of mine, I'm gonna let it shine." Most of us have sung this song since we were kids, right? We shine our light before people, and they can't help but notice it. They see that we live differently, love deeply, and light up darkness.

Our lives are like bonfires on cool fall nights. People will leave the comfort of the indoors, step out into the cold, and draw near the warm glow of a well-made bonfire. There is enough light and heat for an entire crowd to enjoy, and the night no longer feels cold or dark. Everyone loves a bonfire, and rightly so. It's a reminder that even on the darkest night, there can still be warmth and light. People congregate around the flames and forget that the chill of fall is upon them.

People are naturally drawn to those whose lights shine. Others enjoy being in the presence of someone who exhibits the fruit of the Spirit. There's no brighter light than love, joy, peace, patience, gentleness, kindness, faith, and self-control shining from within a person. Others will see it blazing like a bonfire in a field, and they will know there is something different about that person. And the difference is Jesus, the Light of the world.

18

Pumpkin Patches

Having then gifts differing according to the grace that is given to us, let us use them.

Romans 12:6

*A*nyone who visits a pumpkin patch in the fall soon realizes there is a wide variety of pumpkins. There are enormous ones that invite a person to carve elaborate designs on their surfaces. There are also pumpkins with flat surfaces that can be stacked, blue and white pumpkins perfect for decorating, and the traditional bright-orange pumpkins. Also, not to be overlooked are the pie pumpkins. They are, as their name suggests, the perfect size and texture to be turned into a pumpkin pie. Your intended use of the pumpkin will determine which pumpkin you choose.

It is tempting to look around, even within our church family, and begin making comparisons. We label individuals based on what we see and the assumptions we make about them. We analyze another person's gifts and talents and, almost immediately, minimize the beauty and value of our own. The truth is that we have all been created and gifted uniquely by our heavenly Father. And the bigger truth is that every gift was given with the intention that it would be used for God's glory.

Paul was clear in his letter to the Romans that there's a variety of God-given gifts. These gifts are given by God's grace and are to be used for God's glory. Paul didn't instruct the Roman believers to compare their gifts, critique them, or complain about them. "Let us use them," he said. There was the assumption that all of the believers had gifts and that there was a way to use them to benefit the kingdom of God.

Just like the wide variety of pumpkins found in a pumpkin patch, we have all been created with a wide variety of gifts, talents, and interests. We all look different and are gifted differently because we've each been uniquely designed to live out God's purpose. Let's ask God to show us how we can begin using all we've been given to point others to Him. Having gifts that differ, let's use them.

19

Leaf Piles

In all labor there is profit, but idle
chatter leads only to poverty.

Proverbs 14:23

hen I was growing up, my family had an enormous yard with massive trees. The number of leaves that would fall every autumn was indescribable. Eventually my brother and I would step outside and realize that every square inch of the ground was covered, and we knew it was time. Armed with our red plastic rakes and the endgame in mind, we would begin the task of raking the leaves.

After a lot of sweat and a few blisters, we would end up with a mountain of dry, crunchy leaves. Then we would back up all the way to the road, run as fast as we could, hurl ourselves into the air, and land smack in the middle of the leaf pile. The air would fill with leaves flying to various places around the yard. My brother and I would laugh as we emerged from the pile and ran back to the road to do it all over again. This fall fun would go on for hours.

We knew that by jumping in the leaf pile, we would cause the leaves to scatter once again. Of course we understood that we would have to rake the yard again when we were through. But not one time did we ever say, "Well, that wasn't worth the effort." The reward was always worth the work. In fact, knowing what fun awaited us, raking the leaves hardly seemed like work at all. It was simply a means to a really enjoyable end.

Scripture teaches that there is profit in all labor. Perhaps our labor is a hard day's work at our place of employment. Maybe it looks like serving our communities, loving our neighbors, or taking care of our homes. Some of us, no doubt, labor in a variety of ways. We can know that there is profit in it all and that our heavenly Father sees every ounce of energy exerted. Just as no child who ever jumped in a pile of leaves regretted the work of raking the yard, no person rewarded one day by God will regret their labor.

The grass withers, the flower fades, but the word of our God stands *forever*.

ISAIAH 40:8

I'm just here for the *cocoa*.

20

Hot Cocoa

Therefore my heart is glad, and my glory
rejoices; my flesh also will rest in hope.

Psalm 16:9

There is nothing quite like a hot beverage on a chilly fall day. It warms a person up in a way that another layer of clothing simply can't. A cup of steamy hot cocoa topped with marshmallows and a little chocolate drizzle makes you happy from the inside out. (Also, a couple of drops of peppermint extract puts it right over the top. You're welcome.) By the time you've reached the bottom of the mug, you're no longer cold. Perhaps you're even a little toasty.

There is a big difference between what the world calls happiness and what Scripture calls joy. Our happiness originates outside of us and comes and goes depending on what is currently happening to us. We get a raise at work? Happiness. We get a flat tire on the way home that same day? Unhappiness. We go to our favorite restaurant? Happiness. Our order gets messed up and the food isn't great? Unhappiness. Just like that, the happiness pendulum swings back and forth.

Joy, on the other hand, comes from Jesus, and it is an inside-out event. It is completely unrelated to worldly happenings. The psalmist declared that his heart was glad, so his whole being rejoiced and his flesh was at peace. Can you see the progression? Just as hot cocoa warms a person up on the inside, and the warmth spreads all over, joy fills the heart of a Christ follower and spreads all over as well. The joy pours out of us, completely independent of whatever trials we may be facing.

When we experience the joy that is available to us in Christ, our whole being rejoices. We are at peace because our joy is unshakable. There is joy whether our day at work is good or bad. We have joy when the diagnosis is positive and when it's negative. We have joy when people let us down, because we know God never will. It's a whole different way of living. Joy is like hot cocoa on a cold day, and once you've experienced it, you'll never be the same.

21

Thanksgiving Dinner

*They came, both men and women, as many as had a
willing heart, and brought earrings and nose rings,
rings and necklaces, all jewelry of gold, that is, every
man who made an offering of gold to the LORD.*

Exodus 35:22

It was all hands on deck when it came time to build the
Old Testament tabernacle. Scripture tells us in Exodus
35 that everyone who desired to give could give, and whatever they had to offer could be used. Everyone came together
and brought whatever materials they had in their possession.
They used the gifts and talents they had been given. There
wasn't a competition over who had the best gift. No one
was comparing talents. From gold to linens to animal skins,

God could use it all. There was a place for the goldsmith, the seamstress, and the farmer all to contribute.

Growing up, Thanksgiving was the day that our entire family on my dad's side came together. Grandparents, aunts, uncles, and cousins all packed into Aunt Nona's house, and the family stories didn't stop until the last piece of pie had been eaten. There wasn't a sign-up list or perfectly planned menu with equal amounts of sweets and veggies. Were you a master at mashed potatoes? Did you make a killer key lime pie or a mean mac and cheese? Whatever you were good at, that's what you brought, and it was exactly what someone else hoped would be on the Thanksgiving dinner table. Were you a terrible cook? Paper goods were always needed. There was a way for everyone to contribute.

The only real requirement for participation in the building of the tabernacle in Exodus—or my family's Thanksgiving feast—was a willing heart. Whoever was moved to give could do so. At Aunt Nona's, no covered dish was rejected, and there was always room in the kitchen for one more. It is much the same for Christ followers today. If we desire to be a part of what God is doing in our families, our communities, and around the world, all we need are generous and willing hearts. Our contributions will all look different because of our unique gifts and talents, but when we offer all that we have in service to His kingdom, God can use it for His glory.

Today I am thankful.

Sing to the LORD with thanksgiving: *sing* praises on the *harp* to our God.

PSALM 147:7

22

Hats, Gloves, and Scarves—Oh My!

The peace of God, which surpasses all understanding,
will guard your hearts and minds through Christ Jesus.

Philippians 4:7

We are quick to take precautions against the cold weather as the summer months end and the fall season begins. As temperatures plummet and breezes begin to blow, we pull out the accessories necessary to achieve and maintain the warmth we crave. We would not knowingly go out into the cold unprepared, so we guard ourselves with hats, gloves, and scarves.

In his letter to the Philippian church, Paul gave them instructions on how to guard their hearts and minds from things such as bitterness, envy, and self-pity. In fact, he mentioned three ways they could protect themselves from those very things. These three levels of protection are like hats, gloves, and scarves for our hearts and minds.

First, Paul said not to be anxious about *anything*. If you're anything like me and your default mode is often to worry, it's hard to imagine not worrying about anything. That diagnosis, that financial need, that painful family situation, that troubling news headline—all of these fall under the category of "anything." None of it warrants our worry. For me, this often means that I will verbally remind myself, "I don't have to worry about that."

Second, Paul said to pray about everything. The best way to stop a bad habit is to replace it with a better habit. So instead of worrying and being anxious, Paul said that our go-to response should be prayer. Our instinctive urge to panic should serve as a reminder to pray. When we stop to pray, we are shifting the weight of that burden off our shoulders and trusting God to handle the situation as He sees fit.

Finally, all our prayers should be filled with thanksgiving. It's impossible to be bitter, envious, or discontent when we begin counting the many blessings our heavenly Father has bestowed upon us. Gratitude-filled prayers result in a peace that only God can give. Prayers to God result in the peace of God. That peace guards our hearts and minds in Christ Jesus, bringing us more warmth than the best-made fall clothing accessories.

23

Fall Fellowship

They continued steadfastly in the
apostles' doctrine and fellowship, in the
breaking of bread, and in prayers.

Acts 2:42

*S*adly, summer often rushes by in a blur. Family vacations (which are usually not as relaxing as we hope), summer camps, and swimming pools fill the days. There is a mad dash to get all the items on the to-do list done. Children try to fit all the fun they can into ten short weeks. Before we know it, September has burst on the scene like an unexpected visitor, and we are wondering where June, July, and August went. We engage in a lot of activities, but we're also a little exhausted by it all.

Thankfully, something wonderful accompanies the arrival of fall. There is this natural tendency to take the time to pause and truly enjoy the people around us. There are hayrides, bonfires, and chili cook-offs. We sit down to carve pumpkins and watch football. We enjoy soups, s'mores, and candy corn. Fall brings with it a desire to spend time with family and friends enjoying food and fellowship. We plan our season less around events and more around people because—let's face it—fall activities are better with friends.

The early church in the book of Acts is described as spending time with one another in fellowship. They were not scurrying here and there, trying to attend every event and take every photo. They passed the hours together studying Scripture, breaking bread, and praying. This continual coming together of the early church made them stronger. They could share struggles while they shared a meal, and they could be refreshed as their bodies were being refueled.

Fall offers many opportunities to come together and fellowship with friends and family. There is something about breaking bread that bonds people. Unrushed time together works wonders on relationships. A lot can happen between the cheese ball and the pumpkin pie. Let's not miss a single chance to gather with our people this season. And let's take our cue from the early church. May we continue spending time together in worship, fellowship, and prayer.

24

Fall Trees

I will restore to you the years that the
swarming locust has eaten.

Joel 2:25

*I*t's always exciting when the leaves begin falling from the trees and blowing in the crisp breezes of fall. We ooh and aah over the myriad of colors. There comes a point, however, when all the leaves have finished their falling, and the trees stand bare. How do you feel when you see the fall trees without their leaves? At first glance, perhaps, they seem empty, as if everything has been stripped away. They are left standing stark on a gray landscape, and, well, they often seem a little sad and alone. They appear barren.

In time, however, those very same trees will begin to

show signs of new growth. Buds will hint at the beauty of things to come. In due time, fresh flowers and leaves will appear, and the trees that appeared dead will spring to life again. So it's important to remember in the cold days of fall that bare is not the same thing as barren.

Life is full of seasons. There are times when we feel things being stripped away from us and we are left standing bare before the world. Others looking at us may see no signs of life and believe us to be barren. But our God is a God of restoration, and no loss goes unnoticed by Him. Many times, what looks like barrenness to the world is only a season of bareness. Our fruitful days are coming, and God is about to do a work in our lives that only He can do.

Through the prophet Joel, God promised restoration to His people. He promised to restore the years the locusts had eaten. These were locusts that God Himself had sent to swarm among them. The Lord knows when things need to fall away from our lives, and we can trust Him also to bring us again to a season of growth and new life. Just remember that whatever the season you're currently in, bare is not the same as barren and that anything stripped away is leaving room for God to do something new.

Pumpkin spice
and everything nice.

Therefore be *patient*, brethren, until the coming of the Lord. See how the farmer waits for the precious *fruit* of the earth, waiting patiently for it until it receives the early and latter rain.

James 5:7

25

Chili on the Stove

I will meditate on Your precepts,
and contemplate Your ways.

Psalm 119:15

God never intended His Word to be a book that we read one time and put on the shelf to gather dust with the novels and biographies. It is not meant to be a one-and-done activity. We are told that Scripture is alive and active (Hebrews 4:12 NIV). It speaks to us in a variety of circumstances, and it speaks differently to different people. That is why we can read the same passage at two different points in our lives and hear the Lord speak something unique to us in each scenario. There is no denying that the more you read God's Word, the better it gets.

It's a little like a pot of chili on the stove. Anyone who has ever made chili knows that you can't just dump it all in a pot, stir it together for five minutes, and serve it. That isn't the way chili works. It has to simmer on the stove for hours for the flavors to all come together in just the right way. The meat must get tender, and the seasonings must release all of their flavors. The aroma must have time to permeate each and every room of the house until everyone is aware that there is chili on the stove. The general rule for chili is that the longer it sets, the better it gets.

Over and over in Scripture we discover this instruction to meditate on the promises and precepts found in God's Word. The reading of it can't be rushed. We are to ponder the wonder of God's ways and spend time contemplating His extravagant love for us. As we take it in over time, God's Word infiltrates every part of our being and permeates every area of our lives. Our hearts become tender and receptive to His instruction. God's Word becomes something we come back to time and time again. Scripture is not something to be consumed and forgotten but instead something to be kept simmering in our hearts like a pot of chili on the stove. The more we go back to it, the more we see things we never saw before.

The leaves are about to show us how beautiful it is to *let things go*.

And all at once, summer collapsed into *fall*.

Oscar Wilde

26

Mums

*"If you bring your gift to the altar, and there remember that
your brother has something against you, leave your gift
there before the altar, and go your way. First be reconciled
to your brother, and then come and offer your gift."*

Matthew 5:23-24

If you have ever purchased a lovely fall mum and placed
it on your porch only to have it turn brown long before
you hoped it would, then you realize there is a proper and an
improper way to take care of a mum. There are, for example,
specific ways to pot, plant, and water a fall flower. If you
choose to care for it willy-nilly, then you will certainly suf-
fer the consequence of dead flowers greeting your visitors
on your front porch.

In an effort to keep my mums a cheery, bright yellow, I asked the owner of the local nursery how to care for them. It turns out that my main mistake in the past was overwatering them. A mum only needs to be watered every other day and should be watered in the morning, so the moisture is absorbed over the course of the day. I couldn't do whatever was convenient or seemed best to me and still expect the desired result. There is a right and a wrong way to care for mums.

Jesus taught His disciples that there was a right and a wrong way to approach God. They were not to worship in any manner they chose. In fact, if a person showed up at the altar with a gift in his hand but a grudge in his heart, he was to lay the gift down and go make peace with his brother. We are often prone to approach God in a far too casual manner. We should examine Scripture to see what it teaches about how we are to worship Him.

How often do we approach God in an incorrect manner? We have probably all been guilty of harboring ill will toward someone when we come to God in prayer or worship. We've probably not considered that this was a hinderance to our worship. We have become quite careless in our interactions with God. He is completely holy, and there is a right and a wrong way to enter His presence. May we come before God this season with pure motives, peaceful hearts, and proper methods.

27

Pumpkin-Flavored Everything

*"By this all will know that you are My
disciples, if you have love for one another."*

John 13:35

*I*t always happens around the beginning of September.
One minute there is nothing, and the next minute,
everywhere you look, there are signs of fall in the form of
pumpkin-flavored everything. There are pumpkin muffins,
pumpkin cheesecakes, and the ever-popular pumpkin spice
lattes. Just the other day I noticed spiced pumpkin pecan
ice cream at the local grocery store. Apparently nothing is
off-limits. Even without a single glance at a calendar, the

prevalence of pumpkin would give the season away in a flavorful way.

Similarly, there should be an abundance of love present in the life of a believer. Love should be evident in the way we treat our neighbors. There should be love in the way we honor our parents. Love should spur us to serve within our communities. Without uttering a word about church affiliation or conversion experiences, the prevalence of love in our lives should make our relationship with Christ abundantly clear. There should be a trail of brotherly love everywhere we go, and no one should be off-limits.

Is our "love for one another" the most obvious thing about us? Would someone watching the way we conduct ourselves and the way we interact with others know that we are disciples of Christ? Is there something about us that sets us apart as different and identifies us as belonging to God? The essence of Jesus' words was that acts and attitudes of love should be as common in the lives of Christ followers as pumpkin spice lattes in the fall. Just for the record, that is really common.

What would it look like if we were all known for our love for one another? How would it change our families, our workplaces, and our towns if we truly loved one another? I believe it can be done. If someone can make pumpkin-flavored potato chips and convince people to buy them, we can make brotherly love the theme of the season. Let's make it obvious that we are Jesus' disciples.

For every creature of God is *good*, and nothing is to be refused if it is received with thanksgiving.

1 TIMOTHY 4:4

28

A Good Book

So He Himself often withdrew into
the wilderness and prayed.

Luke 5:16

Fall is the perfect time to catch up on your reading. Is there anything better than a hot cup of coffee and a good book on a cold and rainy day? No, there isn't. There is something wonderful about being able to step away from the hustle and bustle of the daily grind and lose yourself in a well-written story. Most of us live rushed, overly busy lives, and it's a good practice to withdraw occasionally to refresh and recharge. While we often feel pressured into staying busy and productive at other times, a drizzly fall day is the perfect opportunity to slip away and be still.

Jesus was often surrounded by people demanding His time and attention. There were crowds desperate for Him to heal them or their loved ones. Some hung on His every word, and they all followed Him everywhere He went. The needs were legitimate, so the people followed Jesus in an attempt to receive what they knew He could provide. The pressure to meet every plea was surely intense. Jesus was often moved with compassion when He saw the crowds around Him. Even so, Luke made a point of telling us that Jesus would, not occasionally but *often*, retreat from the crowds to spend time in prayer. He stepped away from the people to be alone with the Father.

If Jesus saw the need for time alone on a regular basis, then we certainly should make it a habit for ourselves as well. We are better able to love and serve others when we take time to refuel ourselves. It's okay, even in the busiest of seasons, to spend some time away from the crowds. To step away from the noise for a moment and enjoy some time alone. Don't feel guilty about withdrawing to be alone with your heavenly Father. And while you're there, a nice cup of something hot and a good story to get lost in may be just what you need.

29

The Front Porch

Be hospitable to one another without grumbling.

1 Peter 4:9

*W*hether they're small, cozy stoops or grand wrap-arounds, I've always had a slight obsession with front porches. Rocking chairs, porch swings, and unique welcome mats make me happy. Wind chimes, monogrammed signs, and colorful cushions all give little insights into the homeowners. Porches have personalities; some say, "No trespassing," while others say, "Come on in." While baskets of spring flowers or bunches of poinsettias are great, nothing beats a front porch adorned for autumn.

A front porch fully decorated for the fall is a beautiful and welcoming sight. It's like a friendly smile or a warm handshake. Hay bales, pumpkins, cornstalks, scarecrows, and other seasonal decor cause visitors to anticipate the warmth of the home's interior. Hospitality should be a hallmark of a Christian's life, and it can begin on the porch. For many homes, the front porch serves as an extension of the living space and sets the tone for the visit. Have you ever considered what your front porch says to guests? Take a moment and try to view it through the eyes of a visitor.

As Christians, we should be known for our warmth and hospitality. The key to Peter's directive, however, is that the hospitality should be "without grumbling." There's the rub for many of us. We do all the right things but not always with the right attitude. Many of us probably have a little Martha in us that tends to grumble when our routines are disturbed or people don't behave as we wish they would (see Luke 10:38–41). While some certainly have the gift of hospitality, which makes it come a little more naturally, we are all called to be hospitable.

Don't worry if you have been a little weak in this area in the past. There will be plenty of opportunities this season to exercise our hospitality muscles. As we open our homes and hearts to friends and family, let's do so with joy. We can leave room in our schedules for unexpected activities and prepare extra food for surprise guests. May we pass on the grumbling this year and do everything with an extra helping of grace.

30

Homemade Apple Pie

*When you eat the labor of your hands, you
shall be happy, and it shall be well with you.*

Psalm 128:2

There is something undeniably amazing about a home-made apple pie. Sure, you could buy one from a store, put it in your own dish, and try to pass it off as your own creation. Or you could buy a can of pie filling and pour it in a premade crust and call it done. I've done both of those things. But take it from someone who knows: people can recognize a home-made pie a mile away. It's obvious when someone has rolled the dough, sliced the apples, and sprinkled the cinnamon with his or her very own hands.

Just so you know, the benefit isn't only for the one eating

the pie. The one who bakes it enjoys huge rewards too. There are elements of pride and pleasure for the one who puts forth the effort and chooses to do the baking. Perhaps it's because we were made in the image of a creative God, but there is a deep satisfaction found in working with your hands to create something that others enjoy. There is pleasure in serving others by the sweat of our brows.

The psalmist said that enjoying the fruits of our labor would provide happiness. There is joy to be had in a job well done. Who among us hasn't, at some point, put effort into something and was able to experience the pride of completing the task? Scripture teaches us that we are rewarded for our labor, and there is honor in working with our hands.

How much time, effort, and mental energy do we waste concerning ourselves with other people's affairs? If we find ourselves with a tendency to meddle or gossip, perhaps we have too much time on our hands. Let's grab some Granny Smith apples and make a homemade pie.

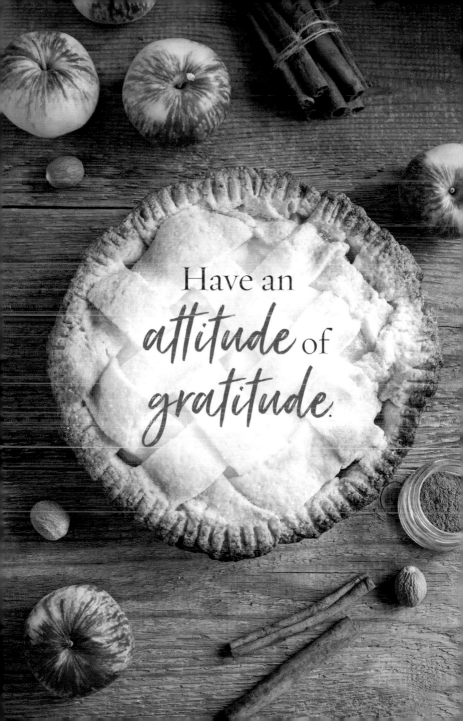

Have an
attitude of
gratitude.

31

Love Thy Neighbor

*If you say, "Surely we did not know this," does not
He who weighs the hearts consider it? He who
keeps your soul, does He not know it? And will He
not render to each man according to his deeds?*

Proverbs 24:12

We are surrounded by people who are suffering,
struggling, and seeking. Our communities are filled
to overflowing with the helpless, hopeless, and heartbro-
ken. Even so, it's easy to get caught up in the busyness of the
season and not even notice other people. How many times
have we heard of someone's need and thought, *I had no
idea*? In Proverbs 24:12, Solomon essentially says, "Don't
think that you can claim ignorance when you stand before

the Lord." In fact, we are to do more than be aware; we are to take action.

Scripture teaches that we are to "rescue those who are being taken away to death; hold back those who are stumbling to the slaughter" (Proverbs 24:11 ESV). We need to do all in our power to rescue those who, through injustice or neglect, are suffering. We need to hold back those who, through ignorance or poor choices, are stumbling down the road to destruction. Regardless of how they got in the position they are in, God's Word is clear that we are to actively and intentionally care for our neighbors.

The beauty of the fall season is that there are endless opportunities to love our neighbors well. There are soup kitchens and food banks that need stockers and servers. There are widows and children who need the gift of a friendly smile and a listening ear. There are families who could use help with groceries, children who need Christmas gifts, and elderly individuals who would appreciate their yards being raked.

There are hundreds of verses in Scripture that speak to loving others, doing good deeds, and being a positive impact on the world around us. Our lives should be filled with the evidence of our love for others. There is no shortage of work to be done, but there is a lack of laborers. Let's ask God to open our eyes to the opportunities all around us to love our neighbors. May we not live blind to the needs of others and then attempt to say, "We didn't know."

Let us come before His presence with thanksgiving; let us *shout joyfully* to Him with psalms.

PSALMS 95:2

32

Friendsgiving

God sets the solitary in families; He brings
out those who are bound into prosperity;
but the rebellious dwell in a dry land.

Psalm 68:6

ne tradition that many people have adopted in recent years is a gathering called Friendsgiving. It's a time when those who aren't related by blood gather together to celebrate and give thanks for the gift of friendship. As someone who has spent many years living far away from family, my heart is warmed by the whole concept of Friendsgiving. It's an intentional choice to celebrate what a person has been given instead of getting caught up in what may be missing. Couldn't we all benefit from that sort of practice?

Anyone who is separated from family due to death, distance, or broken relationships knows that the sting of loss is particularly sharp during the fall and holiday season. It can seem as if you're the only one alone, but we would be shocked at how many people aren't surrounded by family. Yet we have this beautiful promise in Scripture that God takes the lonely and sets them in a family of His making. It may be coworkers, neighbors, fellow students, or a church community. People we never would have expected suddenly become an integral part of our lives.

Some of the greatest gifts God bestows on us are the people He places in our lives. Our Father sees us in our solitude, is aware of every loss, and knows how to rescue the godly from trials (2 Peter 2:9 NIV). One way He often chooses to rescue us is through friends. How often have we had a friend walk through a trial with us? Share their story? Simply sit with us? We call them friends, but could it be that God calls them family?

Before allowing losses to become the theme of our season, we can make a list of all the people God has strategically placed in our lives. Maybe we thought it was a coincidence that we moved in next to someone who became a dear friend. Or that our new coworker had such similar interests. Let's take a moment and recognize the family God has intentionally created for us. Then we can invite them all together for Friendsgiving.

5 Ways to Give Back

* **Buy groceries** for a family in need

* Volunteer at a food bank

* Visit a nursing home

* Invite someone to your family's Thanksgiving

* Send **cards of gratitude** to people who have blessed you

33

Roasted Pumpkin Seeds

I want you to know, brethren, that the things which happened to me have actually turned out for the furtherance of the gospel.

Philippians 1:12

What is the strangest fall treat you've ever made or tasted? For me, it was the first time I saw someone roast pumpkin seeds. My brother and I spent many an afternoon scooping the seeds and strings out of the insides of pumpkins. It was always done on a porch covered in newspapers so that all of the gunk could be properly contained and discarded. Because that's what one does with such unpleasantness. Never did I think that any of the things I dug out of the pumpkin could serve any purpose.

Then, at some point, it was revealed to me that pumpkin seeds were edible. I didn't believe it when someone mentioned it, but after looking into it, I learned that eating pumpkin seeds was really a thing. It turns out that with a simple wash, a quick boil, your favorite seasoning, and a little time in the oven, pumpkin seeds are transformed from gunky garbage to tasty treat. Who would have ever thought it? The transformation is amazing and well worth the effort. It turns out that something good can come from the gunk.

When we look at our lives, we often view certain parts as "gunk" that would be best if discarded. It's hard to see how any good could come from our pain, and we would prefer to keep it properly contained and out of sight. After all, what purpose could it possibly serve? Shouldn't we dispose of it like the seeds from deep within a pumpkin?

Paul penned his letter to the Philippians while sitting deep within a prison cell. He was more than familiar with less-than-pleasant scenarios. He was able to see purpose in what were, no doubt, very unpleasant circumstances. Paul understood that his pain was being used to spread the gospel. God was doing something good with the gunk in Paul's life, and He can do the same with us. Our painful seasons can be a source of strength and encouragement to others. Our pain is not in vain. Something good *can* come from the gunk.

Sweater weather

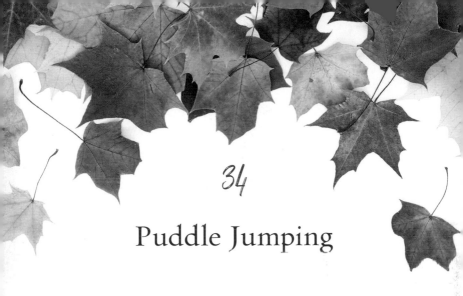

34

Puddle Jumping

For our boasting is this: the testimony of our
conscience that we conducted ourselves in
the world in simplicity and godly sincerity,
not with fleshly wisdom but by the grace of
God, and more abundantly toward you.

2 Corinthians 1:12

If you ever want to bring an amazing amount of joy to a small child, allow them to jump in a rain puddle. Let them get a running start, jump, and land with both feet. The only thing better than the splash will be the laughter. Then, if you want to increase the pleasure tenfold, jump with them. You won't regret it. In a world where bigger is mistaken for better and everything has become complicated, many of us find ourselves craving a simpler way of living. Puddle jumping is a great place to begin.

Imagine all the things Paul had experienced in his life. The people he had met, the places he had been, and the lives he had touched. Consider all the things he had escaped: imprisonments, beatings, and shipwrecks. Yet he did not consider any of those things to be worthy of boasting about. Through it all, he conducted himself with simplicity and sincerity. He knew how to enjoy and be content with the simple things in life. It was, in fact, something boastworthy to him.

What could we do to slow things down just a bit? How can we enjoy more simplicity in our day-to-day living? Perhaps we decline some social invitations and enjoy some cider on our sofas instead. Maybe we participate in a fun fall activity without feeling the need to post about it online. It might be a dance party in the kitchen to some Christmas tunes, a long soak in the tub with a good book, or a good conversation with a friend.

There are countless joys to be found in the simplest of things. Let's listen to the rain. Stop to watch a sunset. Let someone tell us their story. Sit in a rocking chair. Or perhaps we should choose to go puddle jumping on a rainy day. Let's take our cue from Paul this season and choose simplicity and sincerity.

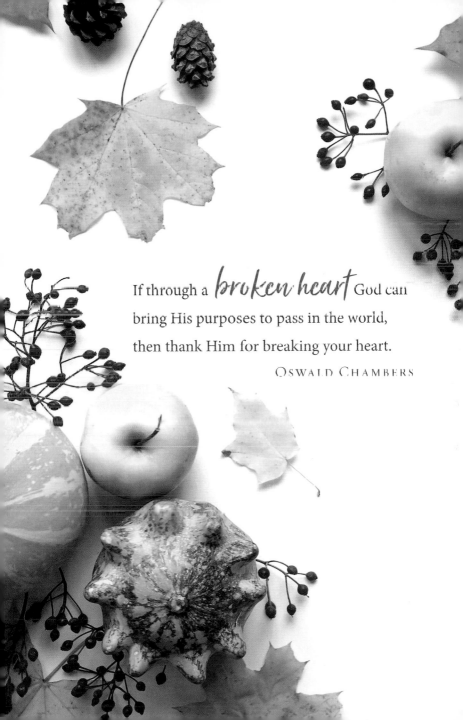

If through a *broken heart* God can bring His purposes to pass in the world, then thank Him for breaking your heart.

OSWALD CHAMBERS

Let everything that has breath praise the LORD. *Praise the Lord!*

PSALM 150:6

35

Shop Local

Therefore, brethren, seek out from among you seven
men of good reputation, full of the Holy Spirit and
wisdom, whom we may appoint over this business.

Acts 6:3

As the early church began to grow in the book of Acts, the number of needs also grew. At one point it was brought to the apostles' attention that a certain group of widows was being neglected in the daily distribution. The apostles, however, did not drop all their responsibilities to tend to this one need. Instead, they summoned all the disciples from that community to come together. From that group they chose seven men to whom they assigned the duty of ensuring the widows would receive appropriate assistance.

The apostles knew that the members of the community were the ones best suited to care for other community members. Who knows better how to engage and meet the needs of the people than those living on the same streets? Our community may be our literal zip code, or it could be the people with whom we identify: military families, stay-at-home moms, or widows. Either way, there are things we can do to minister to the people around us. What do our communities need from us?

One practical way we can support and encourage those around us is to patronize local businesses. Locally owned salons, restaurants, and stores are the lifeblood of small towns. By spending our money in small, family-owned businesses, we are helping our communities and the families within them thrive. Ask around and you'll discover local businesses that offer amazing products and services. It is a simple, hands-on way to love our neighbors and make a difference in the places we call home.

Let's seek out local businesses this fall. Who makes autumn decor by hand? Who grows and sells their own mums? What about local, family-run pumpkin patches and corn mazes? Perhaps we attend local fall activities instead of going to the biggest event in town. There are ways to enjoy the fall, continue traditions, and still bless our communities by shopping local. We know best what our community members need, and that is our support.

But first, *S'mores*.

36

Family Traditions

A story went around several years ago about a woman who, every time she made a pot roast, would cut off about an inch from each end before putting it in the baking dish. One year her husband asked her why she removed the ends, and she replied, "That's how my mom always did it. It makes it taste better." So the next time his mother-in-law was in town, the man asked her about the mysterious step in the pot roast recipe. The woman replied, "Oh, I just never had a big enough pan." And so a tradition began.

Every family has its own ways and traditions. My family makes the same dishes for the holidays. We use Grandma Ruby's green mixing bowl every time we bake someone a birthday cake. No matter how far south we move, we still make bread stuffing—instead of cornbread dressing—for the turkey. Family traditions have a way of reminding us of where we come from and who has been a part of our stories along the way.

Paul taught the early church to hold fast to the traditions they were taught either by letter or in person regarding God. They were to remember the statutes of Scripture and the guidelines for godly living. The importance of prayer, baptism, and the Lord's Supper were to be passed on to their children and grandchildren. The Word of God was to be taught and revered in their homes when they sat down and when they rose up.

What traditions do we hold fast to in our lives? Are we more concerned with the proper way to make a deviled egg than we are with spiritual disciplines? In years to come, when we are no longer physically present, what will future generations say about us and our ways? Let's be certain we are passing on the traditions that truly matter. May they know what we believed to be true of God and that we lived out the gospel that we claimed to believe.

Continue earnestly
in *prayer*, being
vigilant in it with
thanksgiving.

COLOSSIANS 4:2

37

Fall Bucket List

Brethren, I do not count myself to have
apprehended; but one thing I do, forgetting
those things which are behind and reaching
forward to those things which are ahead . . .

Philippians 3:13

ew seasons have a way of instilling within us a fresh resolve to create new memories while still continuing old family traditions. We feel the need to do all the things available to or expected of us, and all too often social media exacerbates the pressure. We see that someone we have never even met is doing elaborate, Pinterest-worthy house decorating, and we feel very inadequate. Why do we do these things to ourselves?

While it would be a mistake to try to do everything, there is something to be said for being intentional about doing some of the things. This also means that we must choose not to do other things. A fall bucket list is a great way to be intentional with our time and effort in a season when the tendency is to attempt too much and enjoy too little. The idea is to make a list of things that you really want to accomplish before the season is over. Maybe it's a professional family photo, homemade cider and donuts, or a hayride. Then be intentional about doing those things.

Paul knew the importance of being intentional. When it came to how he lived his life, he told the Philippian believers, "This is what I do." He chose to forget the things that were behind him. He let go of any mistakes he had made (of which there were many) or opportunities he had missed. Any wrongs committed against him (of which there were many). All of it he intentionally let go. That isn't easy to do, but it freed him up to do the next thing.

Then he chose to reach forward to the things that were ahead. This required him to focus on the things that mattered and to choose only those things that assisted him in his pursuit of Christlike living. This meant that there were things he couldn't do and places he couldn't go. The same is true for us. We must be intentional about reaching only for those things that honor the Lord and bring us joy this season. Let's leave the rest behind.

Pumpkins, *cider*, and corn mazes . . .

38

Surprises

As it is written: "Eye has not seen, nor ear heard,
nor have entered into the heart of man the things
which God has prepared for those who love Him."

1 Corinthians 2:9

*F*all begins a beautiful season of surprises. There is something about this time of year that makes people giddy with excitement and eager to surprise the people they love. Is there anything better than a knock at the door and an unexpected loved one on the other side? If it has ever happened to you, or if it's ever been you on the other side of the door, then you know the joy that comes with such an unexpected gift.

When it comes to surprises, however, nothing can beat what our Father has in store for us in heaven. Paul told the

Corinthian believers that whatever they could conjure up in their minds wouldn't even come close. The most beautiful view they had ever seen could not compare. The most melodic sound that ever reached their ears would fall far short. The scent of cinnamon and the taste of pumpkin, though absolute delights, will pale in comparison.

Sometimes we envision heaven as a slightly better version of our lives here on earth. Maybe the weather will be nicer, we will have better hair, or our joints won't ache anymore. We think life here is good, but life there will be great. Perhaps brussels sprouts will be bad for you and butter pecan ice cream will be a cure-all. The reality, though, is that heaven is incomparable, indescribable, and infinitely better than anything we've ever seen, heard, or even imagined here on earth.

God has gifts in store for His children that we simply cannot even fathom. There are surprises awaiting us that are greater than any guest at the door or gift under the tree. God has an unlimited storehouse of good things that are better than peanut butter cups shaped like pumpkins or trees. I know, it's hard to imagine. He knows how to give these good things to His children, and He longs to lavish them on us. We can prepare to be surprised by the many surprises God has prepared for us.

39

An Afternoon Nap

"Six days you shall work, but on the
seventh day you shall rest; in plowing
time and in harvest you shall rest."

Exodus 34:21

Work was not a consequence of sin; it was a gift from God to His people. We were created on purpose and with a purpose. If you've ever been in a situation where you couldn't work, you know that it doesn't feel good not to be able to contribute. Work was a part of God's design for our lives. It was also always God's intention that His people would experience regular periods of rest from their work. He did not rest on the seventh day because He was weary. Our heavenly Father does not grow tired (Isaiah 40:28). He rested in order to set an example for His children, who would often grow weary.

The fall season, with all its colors and cool breezes, can also bring with it craziness, commotion, and busy calendars. If we fail to rest periodically, we will become overwhelmed by the additional festivities and responsibilities of the holiday months. It doesn't take much for our to-do lists to take over our lives. An occasional afternoon nap will do wonders for the body and spirit, but we have to be willing to allow ourselves the opportunity to rest.

Our Creator, who breathed life into us, knew that our bodies would require rest. It was not a suggestion, but an instruction for our benefit. "You shall rest," Scripture tells us. Deep inside, we know that we need it. Instead, we work harder, drink more caffeine, and stay up later. There is the "fear of missing out" epidemic, and we worry entirely too much about what others will say when we should be concerned with what God has already said.

We don't have to feel guilty for saying no to some things. It's okay to step back and let someone else handle tasks and responsibilities. There is no better way to rest than to take a nice nap on a cold fall afternoon. This means that the next time you experience a dreary day, and you feel like a nap would do you good, you should take yourself up on that opportunity.

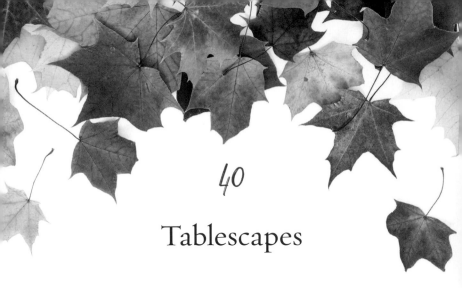

40

Tablescapes

My voice You shall hear in the morning, O LORD; in the morning I will direct it to You, and I will look up.

Psalm 5:3

*I*t takes only a moment of flipping through a magazine or scrolling through social media this time of year to see an abundance of tablescapes. Whether your tastes run formal, casual, or somewhere in between, there is a decor option for you. My mother's favorite room in the house was the dining room. The table was always prepared with a linen tablecloth, a beautiful centerpiece, and nice dishes. As a child, I never understood the concept of presetting the table. But as an adult, I see it differently.

It's possible that some people set nice tablescapes simply

for their beauty. For me, however, the purpose of creating a beautiful dinner table is to send a message to guests. A table full of plates and silver says, "I've been expecting you." It tells someone that their presence is desired. It's such a great feeling to know that someone is eagerly anticipating your arrival.

As David prayed the words of Psalm 5, he gave two key elements to prayer. First, he declared that he would, in fact, spend time communicating with the Lord. "You shall hear my voice," David promised the Lord. In essence, he was telling God, "You can expect me." Are we so consistent in our prayer lives that God can expect to hear from us?

Second, David expected the Lord to show up when he prayed. As he spoke the words, he was already anticipating an answer from God. David prayed and then expected a response from his heavenly Father. Do we expect God to show up when we pray?

Let's live and pray with an expectation of His presence. If Jesus were to show up today, let's make sure we are living in a way that shows we were anticipating His arrival. Let's make sure He has a seat at the table.

If we complained less and

were more thankful, we would

be *happier*, and God

would be more *glorified*.

Charles Spurgeon